Inventors and Creators

Walt
Disney

Other titles in the Inventors and Creators series include:

Alexander Graham Bell
Thomas Edison
Albert Einstein
Henry Ford
Benjamin Franklin
Jim Henson
J.K. Rowling
Jonas Salk
Dr. Seuss
Steven Spielberg
The Wright Brothers

Inventors and Creators

Walt
Disney

Don Nardo

KIDHAVEN
PRESS™

THOMSON
GALE

San Diego • Detroit • New York • San Francisco • Cleveland
New Haven, Conn. • Waterville, Maine • London • Munich

© 2003 by KidHaven Press. KidHaven Press is an imprint of The Gale Group, Inc., a division of Thomson Learning, Inc.

KidHaven™ and Thomson Learning™ are trademarks used herein under license.

For more information, contact
KidHaven Press
27500 Drake Rd.
Farmington Hills, MI 48331-3535
Or you can visit our Internet site at http://www.gale.com

LIBRARY OF CONGRESS CATALOGING-IN-PUBLICATION DATA

Nardo, Don, 1947–
    Walt Disney / by Don Nardo.
        p. cm.—(Inventors and creators)
    Summary: Discusses the life of Walt Disney, including his early childhood, education, interests, the creation of Mickey Mouse, and the development of the Disney theme parks.
    Includes bibliographical references and index.
    ISBN 0-7377-0958-8 (hardback : alk. paper)
    1. Disney, Walt, 1901–1966—Juvenile literature. 2. Animators—United States—Biography—Juvenile literature. [1. Disney, Walt, 1901–1966. 2. Motion pictures—Biography.] I. Title. II. Series.
    NC1766 .U52 D532 2003
    791.43'092—dc21

    2002001834

Printed in China

Contents

Chapter One

The Birth of Mickey Mouse

The name Disney has become legendary. The man behind the legend, Walt Disney, left behind an incredible legacy, or list of achievements, when he died in 1966. It includes thousands of cartoons; hundreds of beloved characters such as Mickey Mouse and Donald Duck; television shows; family and adventure movies; and thrill-packed theme parks attended by millions of people. In every corner of the globe, Disney's trademark—his signature—has come to stand for heartwarming fun and make-believe. Disney may have been the greatest entertainer of the twentieth century. He was certainly the most creative and successful. And the story of his rise from poor beginnings to fame and fortune is truly inspiring.

Boyhood on a Farm

Walter Elias Disney was born in Chicago on December 5, 1901. He was the fourth son of Elias Disney, a building contractor, and his wife, Flora. Elias had always dreamed of being a farmer. So in 1906 he moved his family to forty-eight acres of farmland in Marceline, Missouri (about 120 miles northeast of Kansas City).

Life on the farm was not easy. Everyone in the family was expected to share in the work of growing apples and plums and raising hogs and chickens. The Disney brothers had many daily chores to do in addition to keeping up with their schoolwork. In spite of the hardships, young Walt loved his life on the farm. He later recalled a "green, rolling countryside" in the spring, when "the apple and plum orchards were just starting to blossom. I thought it was a beautiful place."[1]

Inspired by Animals

Another thing Walt Disney enjoyed about living on the farm was being close to so many barnyard animals. He often thought of these creatures as friends, each with a distinct personality. In fact, it was the boy's love of animals that first got him interested in drawing. One day at the age of six he felt the urge to draw a picture of Porker, a huge sow. Because Walt's family was so poor, though, there was no drawing paper available. Already a creative thinker, Walt improvised. He dipped a brush in some tar and sketched—on the side of the farmhouse— a drawing of Porker.

Young Walt searched everywhere for other materials to draw on. He even resorted to sketching on toilet paper. In time, these toilet paper drawings caught the eye of his Aunt Margaret. She recognized the boy's

Disney carefully looks over his drawings for the animated film *Bambi*.

© Disney Enterprises, Inc.

talent and gave him some art paper and a set of colored pencils. Thrilled with the gift, Walt drew every building and animal he saw.

Art Student

These happy days on the farm soon ended, however. In 1911 Elias Disney moved the family again, this time to nearby Kansas City. He bought a newspaper delivery business. And he put nine-year-old Walt and Walt's eighteen-year-old brother, Roy, to work. The brothers had to get up every morning at 3:30 to deliver the *Kansas City Star* door-to-door, no matter how bad the weather.

Young Walt still had an overwhelming urge to express himself through drawing. And he was overjoyed when his father finally allowed him to take formal art lessons. In 1916 at age fourteen, the boy enrolled in the Kansas City Art Institute.

Kansas City Film Ad Company

Soon an unexpected event interrupted Disney's art studies. In 1917 the United States entered World War I and the patriotic young man wanted to help his country. But he was underage. So he altered his birth certificate to make himself older and managed to enlist in the Red Cross. For nine months he drove ambulances in war-torn France.

In 1919 Disney returned home to Kansas City. He landed a position as an apprentice illustrator for an agency that produced catalogs. There he met Ub Iwerks, a shy young man of Dutch descent who was also working as an apprentice. The two young men became good friends. And it was not long before they saw a notice for a job at the Kansas City Film Ad Company. The firm made short, animated commercials for various products and ran them along with the movies at local theaters. Disney got the job; and only a few months later the company hired Iwerks, too.

Disney (left) strums his ukulele on the beach as his brother Roy records the moment on film.

Laugh-O-Grams

Disney was thrilled at the chance to learn about film animation. But he quickly mastered the simple methods used at the Film Ad Company and became bored with making commercials. He was convinced that he could produce comedy cartoons as good as those shown in movie theaters. So he borrowed a camera. And he and Iwerks began doing their own animation at night.

The result was a short, animated film containing brief jokes such as those in newspaper cartoons. Disney sold the film to a local movie house. Then he quit his job at the Film Ad Company and set up his own company, calling it Laugh-O-grams. Ambitious and hardworking, he began work on more complex and difficult projects. The first consisted of a series of six updated fairy tales, among them *Cinderella, Little Red Riding Hood,* and *Puss in Boots.* Disney hired salespeople to promote the cartoons to theaters in other cities. And within months the cartoons played in Philadelphia, Chicago, and Kansas City.

Early in 1923 Disney tackled his most ambitious project to date. He made a version of *Alice in Wonderland* that combined animation with live-action footage. A human actress playing Alice interacted with cute cartoon animals. The short film was highly entertaining. But it had cost so much money to make that Disney was broke. He was unable to raise any more money in Kansas City; so later that year he decided it was time to take another big risk.

Success with *Alice*

That risk was to move to Hollywood, on the outskirts of Los Angeles. While looking for work at the local film studios, he sent a copy of his *Alice* film to Margaret J. Winkler, a New York film distributor. He knew that if he was lucky enough to sign a contract with her, his films would be shown all around the country.

Winkler soon wrote back saying that she liked *Alice* well enough to offer him a deal. She ordered six *Alice* cartoons, to be delivered at the rate of one per month. She also promised to pay $1,500, a large sum at the time, for each film.

Disney persuaded his brother Roy, who had also moved to the Los Angeles area, to handle the financial end of the business. And they rented an office for $35 a month. This marked the modest beginning of the Disney Studio. During the next two years the *Alice* shorts became widely popular. And as Margaret Winkler continued to order more of them, Walt Disney hired more artists and built a larger studio. In 1926 he wisely gave up his own drawing duties. From then on he devoted all his creative talents and work life to supervising his employees.

Marrying Lillian

Meanwhile, Disney's private life was changing, too. In July 1925 he married his secretary, Lillian Bounds. They enjoyed a long and happy relationship and raised two daughters—Diane and Sharon. Lillian understood her husband's devotion to his work as well as to his family; she did not complain when he spent most of his time at the studio.

By 1927 that studio had made almost sixty *Alice* shorts, all of which had turned a profit. But Disney had grown tired of making films that combined animation and live action. He longed to make all-cartoon films again. So he invented a cartoon character—Oswald the Lucky Rabbit. Oswald became the friendly hero of a series of zany comic adventures. After seeing the *Oswald* films, animators, critics, and audiences alike took note of the Disney name. They recognized him as a talented new voice in the cartoon industry.

An advertisement for *Alice* illustrates several of the cartoon's adventurous characters. *Alice in the Jungle* was one of many successful shorts.

Mickey's Big Debut

Not long afterward, Disney created another cartoon animal that replaced Oswald and went on to become the most famous animated character in history. There are several accounts of how Mickey Mouse was born. According to one, Disney first named him Mortimer. But Lillian objected, saying that Mortimer did not sound right for a lovable cartoon character. So Disney changed the mouse's name to Mickey.

It so happened that Mickey appeared at about the same time that the first sound movies were being made. Many filmmakers thought sound was a temporary fad.

Mickey Mouse, dressed as Steamboat Willie, meets a later version of himself.

But Disney recognized that it was the way of the future for all films. So at great expense he rushed a Mickey Mouse cartoon—*Steamboat Willie*—into production. He wanted the characters to growl, squeak, whistle, and talk, a feat very difficult to accomplish at the time. The artists had to find a way to synchronize, or match, the drawn pictures with the sound. They solved the problem by marking the film at each point where they wanted a sound effect.

The short film (or "short") debuted on November 18, 1928, in New York City. Immediately popular with the public, it then opened in theaters across the country and overseas and became a huge financial success. Once more, Disney had taken a big risk that paid off.

But he still was not satisfied. He knew that adding sound was only one way to improve the quality of cartoons. At the time, no one could have imagined that he was about to revolutionize the art of film animation completely and forever.

Chapter Two

Disney and Animation's Golden Age

Before *Steamboat Willie*'s 1928 debut, film cartoons were short, silent, black-and-white, and relatively crude looking. In the twelve years that followed, Walt Disney transformed, or changed, the animated film into an advanced form of artistic expression. At a seemingly impossible pace, he and his artists introduced one innovation, or new idea, after another. This achievement was so important that that highly creative period became known as the Disney Era. It is also often called the golden age of film animation.

New Ideas

The golden age began with Mickey Mouse. The Mickey shorts that followed *Steamboat Willie* were so successful that money began to pour in to the Disney Studio. But Disney immediately used up these profits to hire new employees and experiment with new ideas and equipment. Roy was a cautious man and worried about spending so much money. He complained to his brother that the profits did not always make up for the huge costs of production.

Mickey Mouse stuffed animals surround Disney. Mickey Mouse products became as popular as the cartoons.

Luckily, an extra source of income helped keep Disney's company afloat. The huge popularity of Mickey Mouse enabled the studio to launch a profitable product licensing operation. Business owners around the world paid for the rights to use Mickey on everything from cups to T-shirts to lunchboxes. Disney also sold licenses to use newly created characters such as Donald Duck, Pluto, and Goofy.

The Silly Symphonies

Meanwhile, Disney continued to make comedy shorts starring Mickey well into the 1930s. At the same time he began to experiment with new ideas in a series of cartoon shorts. They were known as the Silly Symphonies. In the first, *The Skeleton Dance*, Disney tried something never before attempted in a cartoon. Rather than try to make people laugh, he combined the visuals and sound to create a mood. In this case it was a scary mood. In the film, four skeletons rise from the grave and dance in the moonlight.

The Skeleton Dance was a big success and inspired Disney to plan more Silly Symphonies. Some introduced new technical advances. One of the most important was the use of color. In 1932, *Flowers and Trees*, about a nice young tree that defeats a mean old stump, became the first successful full-color cartoon. The short proved very popular with moviegoers. And it won the first Academy Award for an animated film. Thereafter, audiences demanded that all cartoons, including those of Disney's competitors, be in color. In this way, Disney forced the entire animation industry to change and improve.

The most famous of the Silly Symphonies was *Three Little Pigs*. Released in 1933, it is the story of three pig brothers defending their homes against a hungry wolf. The short demonstrated that music could be as important in a cartoon as the characters. Disney hired songwriter Frank Churchill to compose "Who's Afraid of the Big Bad Wolf?" The song became an international hit. After that the public identified the film with the song and vice versa; and nearly all of Disney's later films featured memorable music.

Another Disney innovation was the development of more realistic-looking cartoons. He wanted to move away from the flat-looking, often jerky animation of the 1920s. So he spent vast sums on new equipment. And one of his artists invented the multiplane camera, a device that made flat drawings look three-dimensional. The result was *The Old Mill* (1937), a Silly Symphony production with animation that looked very realistic.

Interesting Story Lines

Besides bringing sound, mood, color, music, and realism to cartoons, Walt Disney was a great storyteller. He saw that a major weakness in his competitors' cartoons was a lack of strong or interesting story lines. Disney made sure that each of his Mickey Mouse and Silly Symphonies shorts had a well-paced plot with a clear-cut beginning, middle, and end. Contrary to popular belief, he did not aim his stories at children. At the time, the cartoon market appealed to audiences of all ages. But he recognized that a childlike sense of humor and wonder exists in every person. And he tailored his stories to appeal to that inner sense.

Disney also recognized that only a fairly simple story could be told in seven minutes, the length of an average cartoon in those days. He wanted to tell longer, more complex stories like live-action filmmakers did in their ninety-minute features. Disney also believed that feature-length cartoons would make more money than shorts.

The First Animated Feature

For these reasons, in 1934 he began planning his first animated feature—*Snow White and the Seven Dwarfs*. Disney originally budgeted *Snow White and the Seven Dwarfs* at $250,000. But his constant demands for better quality caused the costs of the project to soar. To Roy's mounting distress, by November 1937 they had spent more than $1.4 million on the film. This was more than four times the average cost of a live-action feature at the time. The studio was now heavily in debt. And nearly everyone, except Walt Disney himself, was sure that the studio would fail.

But to the surprise of many, another of Disney's big risks paid off. *Snow White and the Seven Dwarfs* premiered on December 21, 1937, to rave reviews. The film critic for the *New York Herald Tribune* wrote: "After seeing *Snow White and the Seven Dwarfs* for the third time,

© Disney Enterprises, Inc.

The wicked Queen holds out the box that must return with Snow White's heart in a scene from *Snow White and the Seven Dwarfs*.

I am more certain than ever that it belongs with the few great masterpieces of the screen."[2] Audiences were equally delighted with the film. And it made more than $8 million in less than a year, a huge box office success.

Pinocchio

Even before *Snow White and the Seven Dwarf*'s release, Disney began planning several other elaborate cartoon features. Among these were *Pinocchio* and *Fantasia*. The first was based on the famous story about a puppet that wants to become a real boy. Like *Snow White and the*

Seven Dwarfs, it is a colorful, exciting, and heartwarming film drawn and animated in a highly realistic style. When *Pinocchio* opened on February 7, 1940, most reviews were glowing. One critic called it a work of pure genius.

Unfortunately, however, *Pinocchio* did not do nearly as well as *Snow White and the Seven Dwarfs* had at the box office. Those people who saw it loved it. But World

Pinocchio shows an astonished Geppetto the donkey ears he grew as a result of his misbehavior.

War II had recently begun in Europe; most moviegoers were not in the mood for fairy tales. Disney hoped that *Fantasia* would make up the money *Pinocchio* had lost.

Fantasia

Disney attained new heights of imagination and artistic expression with *Fantasia*. In 1937 he had started work on an ambitious Silly Symphonies short. Titled *The Sorcerer's Apprentice*, it utilized French composer Paul Dukas's classic music of the same name. In the story, a magician's helper, played by Mickey Mouse, gets into trouble by meddling in his master's magic. Disney's brilliant idea was to make the visuals match an existing piece of music instead of writing new music to fit the plot of the cartoon. Disney eventually expanded the short into a feature film with seven other animated sequences. He set each, without dialogue or narration, to the music of a different classical composer.

When *Fantasia* opened in November 1940, it was a financial disappointment. With the war in Europe worsening, many people were still not in the mood for light entertainment. Artistically, however, the film was a triumph. Disney had carried cartoon special effects and realism as far as they could go at the time.

Setting Industry Standards

Indeed, *Fantasia* marked the height of the golden age of animation. In only twelve years, Disney had transformed the animated film from a short, silent string of visual gags into a true art form. Not surprisingly, other animators felt

Disney's influence. They adopted the techniques he had introduced. So the quality of all animated films increased dramatically in the 1930s. But none could seriously compete with Disney; no one had his money or resources, and few had his imagination. In the years to come, he would continue to set the standards for the cartoon industry.

Chapter Three

King of the Television Frontier

For a long time Walt Disney devoted all his time and money to the big screen and gave little thought to the small screen. Throughout the 1940s and into the 1950s, he continued to make high-quality cartoon features. These included *Bambi* (1942), *Cinderella* (1950), *Alice in Wonderland* (1951), and *Peter Pan* (1953), all masterpieces. He also began producing live-action adventure films, such as *Treasure Island* (1950) and *20,000 Leagues Under the Sea* (1954). During these years he watched with interest as the new medium of television gained popularity. And he found himself constantly beset by television executives. They offered him large sums of money to show his world-famous cartoons on their stations. But he did not feel that television showed much promise. The screens were small; the images were often flat or distorted; and the programs were broadcast only in black and white. Television just did not seem the proper showcase for presenting his high-quality films.

Disney finally changed his mind about television because he desperately needed money. He was planning his first theme park—Disneyland. And the project was going to be enormously expensive to build. He decided that if the television people would give him the money he needed, he would find a way to adapt to the new medium. As it turned out, he did more than simply adapt to television; he conquered and for many years dominated it. Indeed, looking back on the history of television, Walt Disney stands out as one of the giants in the medium.

Disney Makes a Deal with ABC

Disney's initial plan for exploiting television was brilliant. Even Roy, who was usually cautious about his brother's new ventures, had to admit it. First, the television people would help pay for building the new theme park. Also, the Disney television shows would regularly advertise the park to the growing home-viewing audience. In addition, the Disney Studio could promote each of its new theatrical films on the television show, which would help boost ticket sales in theaters.

In 1953 Disney set his plan in motion by making a deal with ABC. Of the three television networks that existed at the time—ABC, CBS, and NBC—ABC was the smallest. Desperate for new viewers, ABC's executives jumped at the chance to sign a deal with Disney. They agreed to pay him $500,000 in cash and to lend him $4.5 million, all in return for the right to broadcast his shows.

The first of these shows, *Disneyland*, premiered in October 1954. To both Disney's and ABC's delight, it was an immediate hit. In fact, many people rushed out and bought television sets for the first time just so they could see Disney's films in their own homes. Thanks to Disney, in a single year ABC was as big or bigger than the other two networks.

Disney speaks to the camera with a few of his friends at the ABC studio.

Space Voyages and Frontier Heroes

The episodes Disney broadcast in that first year were extremely varied. As planned, there were periodic progress reports on the building of Disneyland. He also broadcast some of his most popular cartoon shorts from the 1930s. One episode showed scenes from *Snow White and the Seven Dwarfs*, while another was devoted solely to cartoons starring Pluto, Mickey Mouse's dog. One of the most popular episodes showed behind-the-scenes footage from the set of *20,000 Leagues Under the Sea*, which was then in production.

One theme that Disney was especially excited about was space travel. At the time, most people considered going to the moon to be impossible. But Disney was optimistic. He correctly guessed that voyages to the moon would happen in the near future. Eager to inspire audiences with this vision, he made three animated episodes about humans in space. These episodes—"Man in Space," "Mars and Beyond," and "Man and the Moon"—had a tremendous impact on the public. Millions of people came to believe that space travel was possible. And the day after the first episode aired, U.S. president Dwight D. Eisenhower phoned Disney personally to say how impressed he was.

Davy Crockett

Even more popular were Disney's television programs about Davy Crockett, the legendary American frontiersman. The initial three episodes depicted Crockett's adventures as an Indian fighter, U.S. congressman, and hero of the Alamo. Most people at the time knew little about Crockett's life and deeds; so everyone involved in the production, including Disney, was surprised when the episodes started a national Davy Crockett craze. The theme song, "The Ballad of Davy Crockett," shot to the top of the record charts. And Disney received hundreds of thousands of letters demanding more shows about the hero in the coonskin cap. Davy Crockett was so popular, in fact, that Disney decided to transfer him to the big screen. He spliced the three episodes together and re-leased them as a movie—*Davy Crockett, King of the Wild Frontier*—which did extremely well at the box office.

Meanwhile, Disney's original television show under-went several name changes in the following years. In 1958, to give the series a fresh look, Disney changed it from *Disneyland* to *Walt Disney Presents*. In 1961 Disney moved from ABC to NBC, which first broadcast the show in color. So the name became *Walt Disney's Won-derful World of Color*. Regardless of what people called it, the show remained widely popular. In fact, it eventually became the longest running prime-time show in televi-sion history.

More Disney Television Hits

Disney's initial and primary television show was not the only one he created for the small screen. There were many others, each having a different audience appeal. Because *Disneyland* attracted audiences of all ages, Dis-ney felt there was also a need for a show aimed specifi-cally at children.

A young Davy Crockett fan, wearing boots and a coonskin cap, reads about the frontiersman.

There was no question about which Disney character would be the focus of the new show. Mickey Mouse was by far the most beloved children's character. *The Mickey Mouse Club* began its first television run in 1955 and made television history. For the next two years, three-quarters of the nation's homes tuned in to the show each day. Featured were animated segments starring Mickey and other Disney cartoon characters. These alternated with songs, dances, and skits performed by a group of real children called Mouseketeers. (Their name came from the Mickey Mouse ears they wore on their heads and the title of *The Three Musketeers* novel.)

Zorro

The Mickey Mouse Club and *Disneyland* firmly established Disney's image as one of the hottest producers in television. And after that, every new show he created was immediately successful. In the late 1950s came Disney's first live-action adventure series—*Zorro*. Set in Spanish California in the 1700s, the show portrayed the deeds of a masked hero who fought for the rights of the local peasants. Other Disney television hits followed, some of which were produced by Disney's studio long after his death. When cable television became popular in the 1980s, for example, millions of families signed up for The Disney Channel. Like the original *Disneyland* show, it presents a mixture of classic Disney films and newly produced programs.

In 1954 no one could have foreseen the major impact Walt Disney would have on television over the course of many decades. Even Disney himself did not expect such tremendous success. At the time, he regarded television as a way to make the money he needed to finance his theme park. Even while he planned and launched his first television show, the park was foremost on his mind. And thanks to television, he had the money to begin building it.

Chapter Four

The Enduring Disney Theme Parks

For many years Disney dreamed about creating a new kind of family entertainment. He envisioned a large area filled with exciting rides, exhibits, restaurants, and other attractions—in effect, a kind of super amusement park. It came to be called a "theme park" because each section would be built around a theme, such as the frontier, fantasy, or the future. Overall it would be a special spot in which a family could spend an enjoyable day away from the hustle and bustle of the real world.

Planning and Building the Park

In 1951 Disney decided he was ready to begin planning and building what would eventually become the world-famous Disneyland. First, he began to visualize the way the place would look. It would be huge, diverse, and colorful; it would have imaginative and exciting rides as well as its own transportation systems to ferry visitors from place to place; and unlike ordinary amusement parks, it would be clean and attractive at all times. In addition, the park would change and grow constantly. "It's something that will never be finished," Disney said, "something I can keep developing . . . and adding to. . . . The thing will get more beautiful year after year."[3]

The next step was to find a suitable piece of land for the park. Disney located a 160-acre tract of orange groves in Anaheim, a small community south of Los Angeles. The site seemed perfect. The climate of the area was warm and sunny most of the year; that meant he would seldom, if ever, have to close down because of bad weather.

Main Street, U.S.A.

After having bought the land, Disney hired construction companies, landscapers, and craftspeople. They began planning the project according to his overall design. His ideas for the layout of the rides and other attractions were unique, logical, and highly effective. Around the outside boundary of the site, he built a full-scale old-fashioned railroad. He positioned its quaint station at the park's main entrance. After passing by the station, visitors entered Main Street, U.S.A., a charming replica of a midwestern American town circa 1900. It had stores, an ice cream parlor, a movie theater, and a firehouse.

While walking down Main Street, visitors could see the majestic spires of Sleeping Beauty Castle in the distance. This was one of several visual magnets. The idea was to position interesting attractions at key points in the park; each would draw visitors from one section of Disneyland to another.

The other four major sections of the park had themes Disney had used often in his films. Sleeping Beauty Castle marked the entrance to Fantasyland. Here, the rides,

Two lucky children tour Disneyland in 1955 with Walt Disney as their tour guide.

attractions, and exhibits were built around beloved cartoon characters such as Mickey Mouse, Snow White and the Seven Dwarfs, and Peter Pan. Frontierland featured an authentic fort, an Indian village, and other western attractions; while in Adventureland visitors rode boats through a real jungle inhabited by authentic-looking mechanical lions and elephants. Finally, there was Tomorrowland. There, visitors could take a voyage to the moon and view exhibits of cars, houses, and whole cities of the future.

Opening One Park, Planning Another

On July 17, 1955, Walt Disney proudly opened the completed Disneyland to the public. Millions of television viewers around the world watched as he dedicated his dream project with these words:

> To all who come to this happy place: welcome. Disneyland is your land. Here, age relives fond memories of the past and here youth may savor the challenge and promise of the future. Disneyland is dedicated to the ideals, the dreams, and the hard facts that have created America with the hope that it will be a source of joy and inspiration to all the world. [4]

Disneyland was an immediate success. More than thirty thousand people entered its gates on opening day alone. And more than 4 million visitors came in the first year. This success story continued through the years.

Though the park was an impressive achievement, its creator recognized that he had made some serious mis takes. For one thing, Disneyland had only one hotel. Many people visited for two or more days at a time. And because the Disneyland Hotel was always full, they had to find lodgings elsewhere. By the early 1960s, Anaheim motel owners were making more than $500 million a

Walt Disney holds the hand of Mickey Mouse in this statue that stands in Disneyland.

year from Disney's guests; and he regretted that he could not cash in on this business.

Even more serious was the problem of commercial building around the park. Disney had not purchased the land surrounding Disneyland. And over the years outsiders bought this land and built inexpensive motels, bars, and restaurants on it. So Disney could not expand his park. Moreover, the crowded, unattractive structures around Disneyland detracted from its beauty.

A Total Vacation Experience

Disney decided to correct these mistakes by building a bigger and better theme park. In 1964, he sent a team of trusted employees on a special journey to Florida. Their mission was to buy as much land as they could. They had orders not to reveal that they worked for Disney. Otherwise, the owners might charge a fortune for the land.

Disney was thrilled when he received word from his agents. They had managed to piece together a tract covering 27,500 acres (forty-three square miles). Located near Orlando, this land was more than 170 times larger than Disneyland.

Disney searched for a name appropriate for the great size of his new entertainment park. He eventually decided on Disney World. (Roy Disney later expanded it to Walt Disney World). As Walt Disney envisioned it, Disney World would feature many of the same attractions as Disneyland. There would be a storybook castle; a Main Street, U.S.A.; an old-fashioned railroad; and all of the more popular rides found in Disneyland. But Disney did not want simply to repeat himself. The Florida version would have several new theme lands. For example, he planned to build a replica of a colonial American town. There would also be many hotels in Disney World. Instead of having to find lodgings outside of the park, overnight park guests could stay on the premises. This would establish an image of Disney World as a total vacation experience.

His Wonderful Legacy

Despite Disney's commitment, the Florida project progressed slowly. The problem was that Disney overworked himself. He tried to plan almost every detail of the new park and manage his huge entertainment empire at the same time. This was just too much work for one person. Even more serious was the fact that his health was failing. He had long been a heavy smoker; his doctors informed him that he had lung cancer.

Disney's health got steadily worse. By November 1966 he was in so much pain that he had to enter a hospital. There, his wife Lillian and daughters Diane and Sharon visited him regularly. On December 5, they celebrated his sixty-fifth birthday at his bedside. His brother Roy paid him a visit on December 14 and was the last person to see him alive. The next morning the doctors phoned Lillian to say that her husband had passed away during the night.

The news of Disney's death stunned and saddened people around the world. He had brought happiness to

Disney and a tiger friend in 1966. His creations continue to entertain and delight the world.

millions. And his passing seemed to mark the end of an era in show business. Most agreed that there had never been, nor would there ever be again, an entertainer quite like Walt Disney.

But many felt that the sadness of his death was overshadowed by his wonderful legacy. Walt Disney World Resort opened in 1971. In addition to the theme parks, Disney left behind one of the largest movie studios in the world; several successful television shows; and an enormous library of films and beloved characters. These and Disney's other marvelous creations live on and continue to bring joy to new generations.

Notes

Chapter One: The Birth of Mickey Mouse

1. Quoted in Leonard Mosley, *Disney's World*. New York: Stein and Day, 1985, p. 27.

Chapter Two: Disney and Animation's Golden Age

2. Howard Barnes, *New York Herald Tribune*, January 16, 1938.

Chapter Four: The Enduring Disney Theme Parks

3. Quoted in Mosley, *Disney's World*, p. 155.
4. The words appear on a plaque located in the Town Square, Main Street, U.S.A., in Disneyland.

For Further Exploration

John Canemaker, *Walt Disney's Nine Old Men.* New York: Hyperion, 2001. A collection of nine short biographies of Disney's finest animators and their contributions to the animation industry.

Gabrielle Charbonnet, *Adventure at Walt Disney World: A Disney Girls Super Special.* New York: Disney Press, 1999. A group of young girls enjoy a madcap romp through the famous theme park. A combination of information and fun for kids of all ages.

Don Hahn, *Animation Magic: A Behind-the-Scenes Look at How an Animated Film Is Made.* New York: Disney Press, 2000. An easy-to-read guide to the steps animators use to produce cartoons, supplemented by many photos and drawings.

Marie Hammontree, *Walt Disney: Young Movie Maker.* New York: Aladdin Paperbacks, 1997. A short, easy-to-read summary of Disney's life and accomplishments.

Charnan Simon, *Walt Disney: Creator of Magical Worlds.* Danbury, CT: Childrens Press, 2000. A commendable short overview of Walt Disney's achievements and legacy.

Charles Solomon, *Enchanted Drawings: The History of Animation.* New York: Knopf, 1994. A splendid, beautifully illustrated synopsis of the cartoon industry in the twentieth century. The text is challenging for grade-schoolers, but they will also learn from and enjoy the many colorful pictures and their captions.

Bob Thomas, *Disney's Art of Animation: From Mickey Mouse to Beauty and the Beast.* New York: Hyperion, 1991. An entertaining, fact-filled journey through the making of most of Disney's animated films, with plenty of photos and drawings.

Index

Picture Credits

Cover photo: © Hulton/Archive by Getty Images

© Bettmann/CORBIS, 10, 13, 27, 30, 35, 40

© Disney Enterprises, Inc./Kobal Collection, 8, 17, 21, 22

© Robert Holmes/CORBIS, 37

© Roman Soumar/CORBIS, 14

About the Author

In addition to his many studies of ancient empires and cultures, historian and award-winning writer Don Nardo has published numerous biographies of important people in history, among them Julius Caesar, Cleopatra, Thomas Jefferson, Charles Darwin, H.G. Wells, and Adolf Hitler. Along with his wife Christine, Mr. Nardo resides in Massachusetts.